Smart or Honest

The Boat of Honesty: A Story About Values in a Stormy World

A mini book inspired by the story of the two friends

Copyright © 2025 by Aurora D'Costa

All rights reserved. No part of this book may be reproduced, stored in a retrieval system, or transmitted in any form or by any means without written permission from the author, except for brief quotations used in reviews or scholarly work.

ISBN: 978-1-923240-16-2

Table Of Contents

About the Author 3

Preface 5

Chapter 1: Smart vs Honest - Who Wins? 10

Chapter 2: The Strength in Staying True... 14

Chapter 3: When the Waves Crash - The Test of Integrity 18

Chapter 4: Reflections in the Wake - What the Storms Teach Us 23

Chapter 5: The Boats That Leave Us Behind 29

Chapter 6: The Boats That Stay................. 36

Chapter 7: The Arrival of Time 43

Chapter 8: The Moral of the Sea............... 48

Chapter 9: The Quiet Strength of the Broken 56

About the Author

Daisy is a psychologist with a deep passion for exploring human values and resilience. She believes that the most meaningful lessons are often learned through stories, a perspective she inherited from her mother, who used to share life lessons wrapped in tales from her own experiences.

Daisy combines her professional and understanding of human behaviour with the timeless wisdom of storytelling, creating narratives that both guide and inspire readers to reflect on what truly matters in a stormy, ever-changing world.

Through The Boat of Honesty: A Story About Values in a Stormy World, Daisy hopes to inspire readers, young and old alike to reflect on their own choices, the values they hold, and the kind of life they wish to navigate. She hopes the story encourages courage, integrity, and thoughtfulness, even when the waters get rough. And just as her mother passed down wisdom through stories, she invites readers to pass it on, sharing the lessons, reflections, and hope found within these pages with others.

Preface

Life is full of storms. Sometimes they are sudden and violent, leaving us disoriented and unsure which way to turn. Other times, they arrive quietly, slowly eroding the ground beneath our feet until we realize we have been tested all along.

This book is a story about choices, values, and what truly carries us through those storms. It is about two friends, Smart and Honest, who face a challenge that exposes the core of who they are. Their journey is not just about survival at sea; it is a mirror for all of us. Every storm we encounter, every challenge we face, reveals our character in ways that shortcuts and cleverness never can.

You will also meet reflections of real life, people who have faced immense hardship yet continued to act with kindness, generosity, and integrity. These examples show us that strength is not always loud, and success is not always measured by what we grab in the moment.

This story is an invitation.

An invitation to pause, reflect, and consider your own compass.

When the storms come, which friend will you be?

Will you cling to cleverness, chase fleeting rewards, or hold fast to honesty, even when it seems unnoticed?

The answer is yours to discover. And it is a choice that shapes not just your journey, but the world around you.

In life, storms arrive without warning. They shake what we think is solid and reveal who we truly are beneath the surface. Some people cling to whatever keeps them afloat. Others hold on to their values, even when the world feels too rough to reward them.

This is where the story of two friends begins.

Smart and Honest grew up, side by side. One prided himself on quick thinking and sharper instincts. The other held fast to sincerity, loyalty, and doing what felt right. They had always balanced each other, until the day everything changed.

One morning, they set out to sea in a small wooden boat. The water was calm, the sky clear, and the day felt simple. But halfway into their journey, a violent storm rolled in. Waves lifted them like toys. Wind tore through the sky. Within minutes, their boat capsized.

As they struggled in the freezing water, a single rescue boat appeared. It had room for only one person.

Seeing the danger, Smart acted first. Without hesitation, he pushed Honest aside and climbed aboard. By the time Honest resurfaced through the waves, the little rescue boat was already drifting away.

The sea carried Honest for hours until he reached a deserted island. Exhausted, scared, and alone, he waited for help. Eventually, a small boat approached. Its name was painted on the side: Happiness.

"Please save me," Honest called out.

Happiness drifted closer, then answered, "I'm sorry. If I take you with me, I may not stay happy." And it sailed away.

Later, another boat arrived, Status. Honest begged again, but Status refused.

"I worked too hard to get where I am. Taking you might cost me everything."

Not long after, a sleek fast-moving boat named Competition passed by. When Honest pleaded for help, Competition only shook its head.

"The world is tough. If I slow down for you, I will fall behind."

A long time passed.

One by one, the boats drifted away. A storm rolled in again, darker than the first. Just when Honest felt he would be swallowed by the sea, an old man appeared in a simple wooden boat.

"Come aboard," the man said gently.

As Honest climbed in, shaky and overwhelmed, he asked, "Why did you save me when no one else did?"

The man smiled. "Because only time can see the value of honesty."

On their way back, he pointed out two boats in the distance - Happiness and Competition, now overturned in the storm.

"Without honesty," the old man said, "intelligence becomes dangerous, happiness fades, and competition destroys itself."

And so, the journey home began.

Chapter 1

Smart vs Honest - Who Wins?

We grow up hearing that honesty is the best policy, yet the world often seems to reward the opposite. Fast talkers rise quickly. Cleverness gets branded as success. People who bend the rules seem to move forward faster than those who stay steady and sincere.

This chapter explores that tension.

What Society Rewards (At First)

- Quick solutions
- Clever shortcuts
- Outmanoeuvring others
- Winning, even at someone else's cost

From the outside, these traits look like intelligence. They look like survival. People who are "smart" in this way appear to get ahead first, just as the friend who grabbed the rescue boat looked like he had saved himself.

But short-term wins often hide long-term losses.

Public scandals show this repeatedly when politicians get caught in lies, celebrities exposed for cheating systems, businesses collapsing after clever manipulations are uncovered. The fall is usually slower but inevitable.

In contrast, honesty rarely creates dramatic victories. It builds quietly:

- Trust
- Stability
- Credibility
- Respect
- Long-term safety

Honest people sometimes watch others pass them by. But they rarely lose everything in a storm.

This chapter sets the foundation:

In a world obsessed with appearing smart, honesty often seems slower, but ultimately stronger.

Think about a time when being "smart" meant bending the truth or taking a shortcut. What did it give you in the moment, and what did it cost you later, even quietly?

Recall a moment when you chose honesty and it felt slower or harder. Looking back now, how do you feel about that choice?

When you imagine success, whose definition are you using - yours, or the one you learned growing up?

Chapter 2

The Strength in Staying True

After seeing the quick wins of cleverness and the slow rewards of honesty, it is natural to feel frustrated. Why does the world seem to favour those who bend the rules, while the steady and sincere often go unnoticed? The answer lies in perspective: the world measures success in flashes and headlines, but life itself unfolds in years, not moments.

Honesty builds a foundation beneath the surface, one that is rarely visible but always resilient. Each act of truthfulness adds a plank to this foundation - small, sometimes unnoticed, but cumulatively unshakable. It allows relationships to grow deeper, decisions to hold up under pressure, and reputations to withstand storms that would sink those built only on cleverness.

Reflecting on this, we begin to see that honesty is not about immediate rewards. It is about preparation for the challenges we cannot predict, about carrying ourselves with integrity when no one is watching, and about being the kind of person others can rely on when life becomes difficult.

We learn that the so-called "smart" shortcuts often bypass the very lessons that create real strength. Cleverness may gain speed, but honesty develops endurance. It teaches patience, resilience, and the capacity to rebuild when setbacks inevitably come.

The reflection becomes personal:

Which parts of your life rely on the fast wins of cleverness?

Which are anchored in honesty, even when it feels slow or invisible?

The answer may guide not only what you do, but who you become.

Honesty, it turns out, is not a tactic; it is a vessel. And when storms come, it is the vessel that stays afloat, carrying not just survival, but dignity, trust, and a legacy that lasts.

Where in your life do you notice yourself staying true, even when no one is applauding or noticing?

Are there areas where staying true feels exhausting right now? What do you think makes it feel heavy?

If you stopped measuring progress by speed or recognition, what would strength look like for you instead?

Chapter 3

When the Waves Crash - The Test of Integrity

There is a moment in every person's life when the surface cracks. It might be a crisis, a betrayal, a loss, or a pressure that builds quietly until it becomes too heavy to carry. When those waves hit, the mask slips. Hardship has a way of showing what someone is really made of, not in a dramatic, heroic way, but in the small choices that reveal their compass. Some people rise with clarity and kindness, even when they are shaken. Others use the chaos to take shortcuts or protect only themselves.

Stress does not create character.

It exposes it.

Integrity is easy when nothing is at stake. Most people can be pleasant when the waters are calm. The real truth comes out when something is threatened - status, comfort, reputation, or control.

That is when you see -

who listens before reacting

who takes responsibility rather than shifting blame

and who stays grounded even when they feel like running from the room.

These moments don't just test people. They sort them.

There is a quiet irony in this. People who lead with honesty are often the ones overlooked at first. They do not push their way to the front, and they do not perform goodness to win attention. They work steadily. They admit when they do not know something. They follow through even when no one is watching. Because they do not create a dramatic spotlight around themselves, their value is easy to miss. In a world drawn to noise, the steady ones are rarely the first to be chosen.

During times of hardship, this can feel like a punishment. Honest people often watch others rise faster, even when the others lack substance. They may wonder if integrity is worth the effort when shortcuts seem to deliver quicker rewards.

But hardship has a long memory. When the dust settles, the people who stayed grounded are the ones others turn to. Their consistency becomes their currency. Their quietness becomes their strength. Their character becomes undeniable.

This chapter is not about glorifying suffering. It is about recognising that the hardest moments sharpen our understanding of ourselves and the people around us. Hardship reveals who acts out of fear, who acts out of self-interest, and who remains steady because they do not know how to be anything else.

For those who feel unseen despite their honesty, these moments are not the end of the story. They are the turning point. Integrity may be slow to show its rewards, but when it does, it carries more weight than anything built on façade.

When the waves crash, you don't have to become someone you're not.

You simply become more visible.

Think of a difficult moment that tested you. What did your reaction reveal about your values?

When you are under pressure, what do you tend to protect first - your image, your comfort, or your principles?

Who in your life has shown you what integrity looks like during hardship, and what did you learn from watching them?

Chapter 4

Reflections in the Wake - What the Storms Teach Us

After the waves have passed, it becomes quiet. Sometimes it is unsettling, almost hollow, as if life is holding its breath. This is the space where reflection begins, where we can finally look back at what we weathered, what we lost, and what, somehow, remained intact. It is here that life lessons seep in, slowly but unmistakably.

When I think about my own experiences, I realise that the storms, those moments of loss, disappointment, or unexpected pressure have been the teachers I didn't know I needed. There were times I felt unseen, overlooked, or even frustrated that shortcuts and cleverness seemed to carry others further, faster. I questioned whether honesty, patience, and steadiness were worth it.

Yet looking back, I notice a pattern:

Every time I acted from integrity, even quietly, it left a mark. Not always immediately visible, but unmistakable in the long term.

These reflections extend beyond moral choices. They touch on the deeply personal, the relationships that survive, the trust that holds when everything else shifts, and the inner sense of self that refuses to break under pressure. I've noticed that when I allowed myself to lean on what I truly value rather than what the world applauds, I emerged from the chaos with something far more lasting than any short-term reward: clarity about who I am, who I want to be, and what truly matters.

It is easy to forget that life is not a straight line. It is more like a river with unpredictable bends and sudden storms. Some days, the water is calm and progress feels effortless. Other days, it crashes, relentless, testing every plank of the boat you are in. Reflection reminds us that even the slowest, quietest vessels are capable of carrying us through the roughest passages because they were built for endurance, not applause.

This chapter is also about noticing yourself in the small, everyday moments. The kindness extended when no one notices. The patience in teaching or listening. The choices to admit mistakes or stand by principles, even when they are inconvenient. These are the quiet proofs of character, the subtle ways integrity manifests long before anyone else sees it.

I have learned, too, that reflection requires honesty with oneself. It is tempting to romanticise the endurance, to claim the victories and ignore the fear, frustration, or anger felt during the storm.

But true understanding comes when we sit with the full experience, acknowledging both our strength and our vulnerability. It is in this honest reflection that we build a foundation for the next challenge.

Finally, reflecting on the storms makes me see a larger truth: life is less about being rewarded instantly and more about becoming the kind of person who can be relied upon when it matters most. The storms are inevitable, but how we navigate them, what we carry forward, and the lessons we choose to embrace define the lives we build.

For anyone reading this, remember when hardship comes, and it will, look not just at what you lose or who moves ahead. Look at what stays inside you, at the values you refuse to compromise, and at the relationships you have nurtured through patience and care. These are the things that matter. These are the boats that remain, long after the noise fades.

Reflection, ultimately, is not passive. It is active preparation for the next wave. And if we choose to carry it forward - wisely, gently, honestly, we find that storms, while frightening, leave behind more clarity, depth, and resilience than any calm could.

After a storm in your life passed, what stayed with you that you didn't expect?

What did that experience teach you about your limits, your resilience, or your needs?

If you could speak to yourself just before that storm, what quiet truth would you share now?

Chapter 5

The Boats That Leave Us Behind

We grow up believing that certain "boats" will carry us through life. We start to believe this, often without question.

Be happy.

Get ahead.

Win.

Keep up.

These ideas become destinations before we even understand what they mean. They look shiny from the shore, almost like guarantees. But the closer we get, the more we realise they are not built to hold us during real storms. They drift away the moment we reach for them with anything heavier than a smile.

The Boat of Happiness

This boat is the one most people run toward first. It promises comfort, ease, and a sense that everything will fall into place once we achieve the right combination of choices. It tells us that happiness is a destination, something we can eventually lock into.

The trouble is that happiness in this form is fragile. It depends on conditions staying perfect, and life rarely does that for long. When hardship comes, this boat does not wait for us. It drifts off, reminding us that a feeling is not strong enough to anchor a whole life. Happiness matters, but it is not a vessel that can hold us through grief, change, or uncertainty. It can visit us, but it cannot carry us.

The Boat of Status

This one looks sturdy from a distance. It is the boat built from titles, validation, and the sense that others see us as successful. Many people spend years trying to climb aboard by collecting achievements, hoping it will give them security. But status has conditions. It stays only as long as people approve.

The moment we falter, lose momentum, or show a side of ourselves that does not fit the polished image, this boat pulls away without hesitation. Status does not protect anyone. It only reflects what others want to see. When life becomes messy or complicated, it is usually the first boat to disappear.

The Boat of Competition

This boat tells us that life is a race, and someone always has to be in front. It pushes us to measure our worth by what others are doing. It can be thrilling in short bursts, almost addictive, but it has no room for vulnerability. The moment we slow down or break down, it leaves us behind and moves on to the next person who can keep the pace.

Competition can motivate, but it cannot comfort. It cannot sit with someone in fear or uncertainty. It demands constant performance, and no one can sustain that forever.

When we rely on these boats, it is easy to feel abandoned when real challenges hit. Not because we failed, but because these vessels were never designed to carry the full weight of a human life. They serve us only when we are light and uncomplicated. The moment we need depth or support, they slip away.

The truth is that we don't lose these boats. They were never ours to begin with. They belong to a world that values appearances more than substance. When we understand this, something shifts. We stop chasing vessels that refuse to hold us and start looking for what actually stays.

Integrity. Connection. Inner strength.

Relationships that grow deeper rather than thinner when tested. These are the boats that do not leave. They may not shine on the surface, but they carry us when everything else fails.

Real stability begins when we let the flashy boats go and choose the ones that were waiting quietly at the shore all along.

Which boats have you trusted that drifted away when life became complicated?

How did you feel when those boats left? Confusing, Painful, Disappointing, or Clarifying?

What did their absence teach you about what cannot hold you in the long run?

Exercises

Map your boats:

Identify which values, relationships, or habits represent your boats.

Storm reflection:

Think about past challenges and which boats stayed, which drifted.

Boat inventory:

Consider what you need to reinforce your steady boats for the future.

Chapter 6
The Boats That Stay

After the others leave, there is a strange quietness. No applause, no pressure to hurry, no shining destination pulling us forward. At first, this silence can feel unsettling. We are so used to chasing movement that stillness feels like loss. But it is in this quietness that we finally notice what never drifted away.

These boats do not announce themselves. They are not polished or impressive from a distance. They do not promise ease or admiration. They are steady, weathered, and often overlooked. They were built for weight.

The Boat of Integrity

This boat does not move quickly, and it never cuts corners. It carries the choices we make when no one is watching. Integrity does not protect us from hardship, but it gives us something solid to stand on when hardship arrives.

When we act in alignment with our values, we are not scrambling to maintain an image or defend a version of ourselves. This boat stays because it is held together from the inside. Even when the water is rough, it does not split under pressure.

The Boat of Connection

Unlike the others, this boat was never meant to be boarded alone. It is built through presence, honesty, and the willingness to be seen as we are, not as we perform. Connection deepens in difficulty. It strengthens when we allow others to sit with us in uncertainty rather than impress them with resilience we do not feel. These relationships do not disappear when life becomes heavy. They lean in. They make room. They remind us that being carried together is different from being carried by approval.

The Boat of Inner Strength

This one is often mistaken for toughness, but it is something quieter. Inner strength is the ability to remain with ourselves without needing constant reassurance. It is built through reflection, acceptance, and the slow practice of trust in our own capacity to endure. This boat does not eliminate fear or doubt, but it holds them without capsizing. When everything external shifts, it remains steady because it is not tied to outcomes.

These boats are not exciting in the way the others were. They do not offer shortcuts or applause. But they do not leave when we falter. They do not disappear when we grieve, change direction, or outgrow who we once were. They are built to carry complexity, contradiction, and time.

Many people never notice these boats because they are too busy chasing the ones that sparkle. Others notice them only after being left behind enough times to stop running. There is no shame in arriving here later. Wisdom often comes after exhaustion.

When we choose these boats, life does not become easier, but it becomes steadier. We stop asking to be rescued and start learning how to stay afloat with what is real. We move forward more slowly, but with less fear of being abandoned by the very things we trusted.

And perhaps that is the quiet reward. Not arriving faster or looking better from the shore, but knowing that whatever waters we enter, we are no longer at the mercy of boats that were never meant to stay.

Which steady boats are already present in your life, even if you don't always notice them?

Who or what remains when you stop performing, achieving, or explaining yourself?

How might you care for these boats more intentionally, knowing they carry real weight?

Reflection

What boats are you still chasing, even though they have already left you once before?

Which parts of your life feel most fragile when things do not go to plan, and what does that say about what you're relying on?

Who remains present when you stop performing, achieving, or explaining yourself?

What stays intact when approval, momentum, or certainty disappear?

If everything external was stripped back, what in you would still be standing?

And finally, if you were to build a life that could hold you in hard seasons, what would you choose to strengthen first?

These are reflections to sit with, not to answer quickly, but to notice over time

Chapter 7

The Arrival of Time

Time shows up quietly. It never rushes, and it never arrives when we want it to. In this story, Time is the old man who walks along the shore long after everyone else has left. He sees what others miss. He notices the people who stayed steady while the world rewarded noise and speed. He is not impressed by the boats that left early or the crowds that ran after them. He has lived long enough to know the value off time and that anything built on shortcuts eventually sinks. What lasts is different. It takes root slowly, almost invisibly.

When Time speaks, he does not use big declarations. He observes. He remembers. He weighs people's actions over days and years, not moments. He knows who kept their word even when it cost them something. He knows who held their values close when pressure pushed them to do otherwise. To him, honesty is not a performance. It is something stronger, something that survives every season because it never depended on applause.

The fascinating thing about Time is that he never rewards people at the beginning. Integrity rarely gets the first win. He does not attract quick praise or instant comfort. People with steady values often feel overshadowed by louder personalities and faster climbers. But Time is not interested in the rush. He waits for life to unfold, and then he steps forward with a kind of quiet fairness. When the storms pass and the boats that once looked impressive fall apart, he turns to the ones who remained consistent. He sees the strength they built in silence.

In this way, Time becomes the great equaliser. He shows that character may not shine early but unfolds over time and it outlasts everything that does shine. The old man understands that a person's worth is revealed slowly, the same way a coastline takes shape and emerges through years of tide and weather. It isn't instant. It isn't dramatic. But it is real.

When people finally look back, they realise something important. The ones who lived honestly were not behind at all. They were building something that could survive. Time is the one who shows this truth. It does not judge by speed or popularity. It looks at longevity. It looks at what remains standing after years of change, conflict, disappointment, and growth.

This chapter is a reminder that integrity is a long game. It does not need to be flashy. It just needs to endure. And when Time arrives, it always sees the ones who chose the harder path, the slower path, the honest path. It recognises them instantly, because he has been watching from the very beginning.

Looking back, how has time revealed the truth about people, choices, or paths you once questioned?

What feels clearer now than it did five or ten years ago?

If time is the quiet judge of character, what do you hope it will say about how you lived?

Chapter 8

The Moral of the Sea

The sea has a way of telling the truth. It strips away the layers people use to impress others and leaves only what is real. In this story, the storm exposes something many of us already know deep down. Intelligence without integrity can cause harm. It can push others aside, twist situations for personal gain or hide selfish choices behind clever explanations. Smart may have saved himself in the moment, but he created a future built on fear and guilt. The sea remembers choices like that.

Happiness, when chased as a possession, behaves just like the boat that refused to help. It looks bright from a distance, but it vanishes when life becomes uncomfortable. Happiness based only on convenience is fragile. It sails away when we need support the most. Real happiness is quieter. It grows from relationships built with sincerity, not from avoiding other people's struggles.

Status is no different. It feels powerful while things are going well, but it disappears quickly when tested. People who cling to status often focus on protecting their image instead of protecting their values. When the storm rolled in, the boat of status cared more about what it might lose than who it might help. That is the nature of shallow power. It is temporary.

Competition might drive progress, but without honesty it becomes destructive. It teaches people to treat others as obstacles instead of companions. The boat of competition left because helping someone else, could mean losing. Many of us learn this message without even noticing. We forget that collaboration carries people further than rivalry ever will.

The sea teaches a different kind of wisdom. It reminds us that the qualities people admire in the moment are not the ones that carry them through a lifetime. What lasts is the inner compass. It is the quiet pull inside that tells us who we are, even when pressure tries to bend us. When we ignore it, we may win small victories, but we lose ourselves a little at a time. When we follow it, we might face delays or disappointments, yet we build a life we can stand in without regret.

The story of Smart and Honest is not just about two friends. It is about the choices we make when fear rises and the world feels uncertain. It is about the values that stay firm when everything else falls apart. And it is about the truth that Time eventually shows us. The people who choose honesty may seem overlooked at first, but they are the ones who create lives that can weather any storm.

After reading the story, which boat do you feel called to step into more fully?

What would change in your daily choices if you trusted that slow, steady values truly endure?

Who could benefit from hearing this story, and how might you pass it on in your own way?

A Mirror Back to the Reader

This story is a mirror, not a fable about strangers. The storm, the boats, and the choices show up in our own lives all the time.

Question:

When pressure rises, who do I become?

Remember to chose honesty, even when it slows you down. Make it clear that character creates a life that lasts longer than any shortcut.

The Sea Never Lies

The ocean reveals the truth about every boat and its value.

Trust that life does the same. Even if the world seems to reward cleverness over integrity, the deeper currents always bring honesty back to shore. Invite them to choose the path that can face any storm.

The Long Game of Integrity

Integrity is a long-term investment.

In the early chapters of life, it does not always look like the winning strategy. But with time, it outlasts everything that was built on fear or ego.

Each day offers a choice: To live only for what feels good now, or to live with tomorrow in mind. Remember, the future you are becoming deserves your care today.

A Personal Challenge - Which Friend Are You?

The story of Smart and Honest is more than a tale about two friends. It is a mirror held up to each of us. The storms, the waves, and the boats we see drifting away - Happiness, Status, Competition are not just metaphors. They are the pressures, temptations, and shortcuts we encounter in our own lives.

When the seas rise, when life feels uncertain, and when the easy path beckons, who do we become?

This is the question the story asks you:

Which friend are you?

Do you act like Smart, seizing the moment and protecting yourself, even if it means pushing others aside?

Or do you act like Honest, holding fast to your integrity, even when the world seems to reward the clever and the ruthless?

Now is also the time to look at your own boats.

Which ones are you chasing?

Which ones will leave you behind when the real storms come?

And most importantly: which values will anchor you when everything else drifts away?

Choosing honesty, character, and integrity is rarely the easiest path. It is slower, quieter, and sometimes overlooked. But it is the path that endures. It is the path that carries you safely through life's storms, the one that will hold you when the world tests you.

So, take a moment…….

Look at yourself in the mirror of this story. Decide what kind of friend, what kind of person, you want to be, not for applause, not for recognition, but because you know in your heart it is the right choice.

Let honesty be your anchor.

Let it guide every choice, every action, and every storm you face.

Because when the waves crash, the boats leave and the storms come, it is character, not cleverness that will carry you home.

Chapter 9:
The Quiet Strength of the Broken

In life, the people who endure the most storms are not always the ones who seem strongest on the surface. Sometimes they are the quietest, the ones who have been broken and rebuilt so many times that they carry a deep understanding of what truly matters. They are the ones who choose honesty when shortcuts tempt them, who extend kindness even when it is inconvenient, and who act with integrity even when no one is watching.

Take a moment to think of anyone who has been marked by loss tragedy, hardship, personal grief, accidents and loss of loved ones. Yet in the midst of this, they choose generosity, humility and compassion. They do not chase recognition or applause. Instead, they quietly give what they can, support others and live by a code that reflects their inner compass.

Like Honest in our story, we know that real strength often comes from a willingness to keep going, to remain kind, and to stay true to our values even when life punishes us for it. The storms will come for all of us. The tempting boats - Happiness, Status, Competition and will appear. And some of them will leave us behind.

But if we cultivate honesty, integrity, and compassion, we create a life that cannot be overturned by any wave. Our character becomes the vessel that carries us through hardship. It is the quiet, steady force that others notice only after the storm has passed, but it is the force that endures.

The following in not meant to be rushed.

It works best when returned to, especially after life reminds you why things matter.

Sitting With the Storm

Before we rush to meaning, fixes, or lessons, there is value in simply sitting with what has been broken. Most people are taught to move on quickly, to reframe pain into productivity. But quiet strength grows in the pause.

Take a moment to reflect on the storms you have lived through.

Not the ones you talk about easily, but the ones that changed how you see people, safety, love, or yourself.

- Write about one storm that reshaped you.
- What did it take from you?
- What did it leave behind?
- Now consider this gently.
- Who were you trying to be during that time?

Many of us discover that in hardship, we were not trying to be impressive. We were trying to be honest. We were trying to survive without losing ourselves.

Ask yourself:

- When things were hardest, what value did I refuse to abandon?
- When did I choose truth over ease, even if it cost me?
- What did I learn about what actually matters?

Strength is not proven by how well we perform when life is kind. It is revealed by what we protect when life is not. The values you cling to during your storm are not accidents. They are your inner compass showing itself.

Close this chapter by writing one sentence that begins with:

"When everything was uncertain, I stayed true to…"

Let it be simple. Let it be honest.

Choosing the Vessel You Live In

Life will always offer tempting boats. Some promise happiness if you hurry. Others promise safety if you compete, conform, or harden yourself. Many look convincing from the outside. Few are built to last.

This is about choosing the vessel you live in.

Instead of asking, "What should I chase?"

Try asking:

"What kind of person do I want to be when no one is watching?"

Reflect on moments when you could have taken a shortcut but did not.

- A time you told the truth when silence would have been easier
- A moment you acted kindly without being rewarded
- A decision that cost you something but let you keep your self respect

Write about one of these moments in detail.

What did it feel like in your body?

What did it cost you at the time?

What did it quietly give you later?

Now imagine a future storm. Not with fear, but with realism. Life will test you again.

It always does.

Ask yourself:

- When that storm comes, what values do I want steering me?
- What would integrity look like for me, specifically?
- What kind of life would feel solid even if recognition never arrives?

Your character is not something you display. It is something you inhabit. It becomes the vessel that carries you through waves that would otherwise break you.

Write a short commitment to yourself.

Not a promise to be perfect, but a reminder of direction.

For example

"When the next storm comes, I choose to stay aligned with..."

This is not about being admired.

It is about being anchored.

Now, as you close this book, remember:

The storms will come. The tempting boats will drift away. But your integrity, your inner compass can never be taken from you.

Choose it.

Protect it.

And let it guide you home.

"When the waves crash and the boats drift away,

let your honesty be the vessel that carries you home."

www.ingramcontent.com/pod-product-compliance
Lightning Source LLC
Chambersburg PA
CBHW070800050426
42452CB00012B/2423